T0012425

RISING SEAS

By Raymond Bergin

Consultant: David L. Fox
Professor of Earth & Environmental Sciences
University of Minnesota

BEARPORT
PUBLISHING

Minneapolis, Minnesota

Credits

Cover and title page, © MathieuRivrin/Getty, © D.Alimkin/Shutterstock; 4–5, © Contact Naomi for Right/APImages; 6–7, © m.malinika/Shutterstock; 8–9, © Ron Niebrugge/Alamy; 10–11, © redtea/iStockphoto; 12–13, © Tracey Whitefoot/Alamy; 14–15, © Tenedos/iStockphoto; 16–17, © Chris Nicotera/Shutterstock; 18–19, © Benjamin Clapp /Alamy; 20–21, © Cavan Images/Getty; 22L, © moosehenderson/Shutterstock; 22R, © aaprophoto/iStockphoto; 23, © Willyam Bradberry/Shutterstock; 24–25, © PJF Military Collection/Alamy; 26–27, © robertharding/Alamy; 28, © TR STOK/Shutterstock; 29, © Alexey Rotanov/Shutterstock, © BrittaKokemor/iStockphoto, © CasarsaGuru/iStockphoto, © South_agency/iStockphoto, © tanyss/iStockphoto.

President: Jen Jenson
Director of Product Development: Spencer Brinker
Senior Editor: Allison Juda
Associate Editor: Charly Haley
Senior Designer: Colin O'Dea

Library of Congress Cataloging-in-Publication Data

Names: Bergin, Raymond, 1968- author.
Title: Rising seas / by Raymond Bergin.
Description: Minneapolis, Minnesota : Bearport Publishing Company, [2022] | Series: What on earth? climate change explained | Includes bibliographical references and index.
Identifiers: LCCN 2021034174 (print) | LCCN 2021034175 (ebook) | ISBN 9781636915586 (library binding) | ISBN 9781636915654 (paperback) | ISBN 9781636915722 (ebook)
Subjects: LCSH: Sea level--Climatic factors--Juvenile literature. | Climatic changes--Juvenile literature.
Classification: LCC GC89 .B47 2022 (print) | LCC GC89 (ebook) | DDC 551.45/8--dc23
LC record available at https://lccn.loc.gov/2021034174
LC ebook record available at https://lccn.loc.gov/2021034175

For more information, write to Bearport Publishing, 5357 Penn Avenue South, Minneapolis, MN 55419. Printed in the United States of America.

Contents

Escaping a Flooded Home 4

Rising Temperatures 6

Melting Ice...........................8

Losing a Reflector 10

Warming Up and Spreading Out 12

Measuring Sea Levels 14

What a Nuisance! 16

Storm Surge! 18

Wetlands Getting Wetter 20

Animals in Danger 22

Heading Underwater 24

What Are We Doing about It?.........26

Battle Rising Seas! 28

Glossary.................................. 30

Read More.................................31

Learn More Online.......................31

Index..................................... 32

About the Author 32

Escaping a Flooded Home

The coastal village of Vunidogoloa in Fiji is a ghost town. In 2014, floods and **erosion** of the land forced villagers to move inland. They left behind flooded gardens and fields. The villagers' drinking water was ruined by the same salt water that destroyed their homes and land.

And these villagers are not alone. People in coastal communities around the world are watching water rise and wondering if they should stay or go. What on Earth is going on?

Several Native American tribal communities in Alaska and Louisiana have been forced to make plans to relocate due to rising seas and flooding. Some are calling them the first U.S. **climate refugees**.

Rising Temperatures

Our planet is warming quickly. This is mostly due to the burning of **fossil fuels**, including gas, oil, and coal. As the fuels power our cars, homes, and factories, they release **carbon dioxide** and other gases into our **atmosphere**. These gases trap heat around our planet.

The extra heat is causing the air and oceans to warm up. Higher temperatures are changing the **climate**, or usual weather, worldwide. Even our planet's coldest, iciest spots—the **glaciers** and ice sheets of the Arctic and the Antarctic—are getting warmer.

The hottest decade in Earth's recorded history was 2010–2019, with many of the planet's warmest years happening in the same time period.

1 The sun's light comes to Earth. Its heat warms the planet.

3 These gases trap extra heat around Earth.

2 Human activities send gases into the air.

7

Melting Ice

As our planet's air and water temperatures rise, the world's glaciers and ice sheets melt. When ice on land melts or breaks apart and falls into the ocean, it is like adding ice cubes to a glass of water. As the ice cubes melt, they increase the amount of water in the glass. Soon, a full glass might even overflow—or water along a coast might come onto land. Higher seas are already beginning to flood some homes and businesses in coastal areas.

The planet's ice is melting more quickly than ever before. In the 1980s, the world's glaciers lost what would be about the same as 6.5 inches (16.5 cm) of water through melting. From 2010–2018, they lost five times as much.

Losing a Reflector

When ice melts away, it starts a cycle that speeds up climate change even more. The white surface of ice reflects the sun's light and heat away from Earth. This keeps the planet cooler. However, the dark surface of the ocean that is left behind when ice melts does the opposite. The ocean **absorbs** the sun's heat. Then, the ocean waters get warmer and cause even more ice to melt. The ice melts into the ocean even faster, and sea levels continue to rise.

Ice reflects 80 percent of the sunlight that hits it back into space. The ocean absorbs 90 percent of the same sunlight. The more ocean surface that is uncovered by ice, the warmer the planet gets.

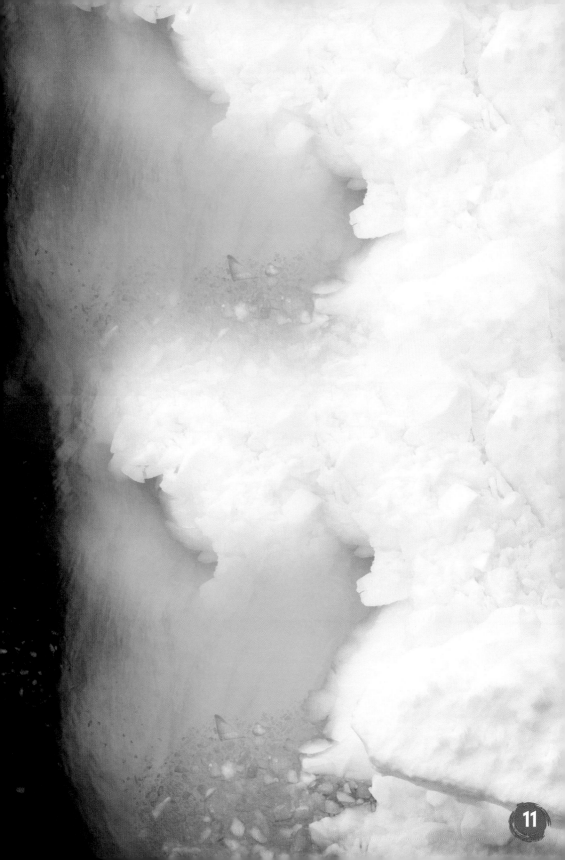

Warming Up and Spreading Out

Warming oceans add to the problem of rising seas. When water is heated, it expands, or takes up more space. So, as oceans get warmer, they become bigger and sea levels rise even more. Along coasts, expanding water can wash farther inland.

This often causes flooding for communities along the coast. In parts of the Pacific Ocean, some small islands have disappeared completely under warming rising seas. Some people on larger islands face regular flooding and may soon have to relocate.

Warmer ocean temperatures are the cause of one-third of the rise in ocean levels over the last few decades. The rest is caused by melting ice sheets and glaciers.

Measuring Sea Levels

How do we know that sea levels are rising? We look at the amount of water in the world's oceans.

Globally, more than one in five people live along a coastline where seas are rising half an inch (13 mm) or more every year.

For years, scientists have recorded the average depth of water in all the world's oceans. That average is called the global sea level. This data shows that sea levels have risen 8 to 9 inches (20 to 23 cm) since 1880. And now the oceans are rising even faster because of global warming. Since the early 2000s, the average yearly sea level rise has been double that of the 20th century.

Scientists measure water levels in many ways. Sometimes they collect data from the ground. Special satellites high above Earth also measure global sea levels.

What a Nuisance!

It's not just the big problems of large floods or the slow trek of water creeping toward land that make a splash. Changing sea levels can also be a **nuisance**. Water along the coast has a natural cycle of higher and lower levels. During **high tides**, the water comes farther onto land, and during low tides the edge is the farthest away.

Nuisance flooding occurs in coastal communities when high tides are especially high. These kinds of floods don't cause major damage. But they can swamp roads, close bridges, cause storm drains to back up, and flood basements.

The number of nuisance floods has doubled over the last 30 years. By 2050, some coastal communities in Texas and Louisiana may see more than 200 days of nuisance flooding a year.

Nuisance flooding can shut down a whole city until the water levels lower again.

Storm Surge!

The most damaging floods are caused by serious storms. Extra warmth due to climate change makes monster storms over the oceans more frequent and more powerful. Hurricanes are forming more often and bringing with them higher winds and more rainfall.

When extra-strong hurricanes hit land and combine with the higher tides of warmer oceans, they create huge storm **surges**. During a storm surge, ocean water floods coastal areas well beyond the usual high-tide mark. These massive floods often wipe away beaches, destroy roads and homes, and take lives.

Almost one out of every three people live along coasts and river **deltas** that are at high risk of flooding. The places with the largest number of people at risk are in China, India, and Bangladesh.

Wetlands Getting Wetter

The flooding that comes with rising seas and powerful storm surges isn't harming only buildings and roads. It's also damaging the natural environments that help prevent floods in the first place.

The plants in coastal **wetlands** store water and then release it slowly over a large area. They can help take in water from storm surges and lessen high-tide flooding. But rising sea levels are drowning some wetlands. When these natural flood barriers are gone, water is able to easily cause more serious damage along the coast.

Just one acre (4,000 sq m) of wetland can absorb 330,000 gallons (1,250,000 L) of water—enough to flood 13 homes in several feet of water.

Animals in Danger

Rising sea levels and storm surges are also harming plants and animals along the coast. High tides are washing away the loggerhead turtle's nesting area along the southeastern coast of the United States. On the West Coast, beach erosion and flooding are destroying the sandy nesting and feeding grounds of a bird called the snowy plover. In the Florida Keys, a rare kind of deer is losing its habitat due to flooding.

Key deer

Snowy plover

Key deer, loggerhead turtles, and snowy plovers are not alone. Rising sea levels in the United States are endangering 233 species of coastal and island animals and plants.

Loggerhead turtle

Heading Underwater

If we don't find ways to slow climate change, coastal areas around the world will get even wetter. Scientists think by 2050, almost 600 coastal cities will likely face a sea level rise of at least 1.6 feet (0.5 m). And they predict sea levels will rise anywhere from 1 to 8 ft (0.3 to 2.4 m) by 2100.

Some scientists predict that large parts of New Orleans, Miami, and Houston will be underwater by 2100. In Brazil, much of Rio de Janeiro may be permanently flooded. And most of Shanghai, in China, may also disappear.

Parts of Asia will be hit especially hard. Almost one-quarter of Vietnam's population, more than 20 million people, live on land that may be permanently flooded by 2100.

The flooding in New
Orleans after Hurricane
Katrina in 2005 showed
how vulnerable the coastal
city is when rising waters
head closer to land.

What Are We Doing about It?

The best way to slow sea-level rise is to slash the amount of heat-trapping gases from fossil fuels we let into the atmosphere. To help, people around the world are switching to cleaner energy sources, such as wind and solar power. Some are trying to prevent flooding and erosion by restoring wetlands and other natural flood barriers. Sand dunes, **reefs**, and **barrier islands** are all being saved. Some cities are even building structures that block or redirect floodwaters.

Waters are rising, but so is hope for solutions. If we all work together, we can turn the tide on climate change!

Tadjourah, Djibouti, in east Africa, fights rising seas by combining human-made and natural flood solutions. Workers there built a 1.25-mile (2-km) floodwall and are also restoring coastal forests that naturally block and soak up storm surges.

The city of London, England, has built flood barriers along the Thames River.

Battle Rising Seas!

To slow rising sea levels and the climate change that causes them, we must cut down on our use of fossil fuels. The less electricity and gas we use, the less heat-trapping carbon dioxide we release into the atmosphere. What can we do to battle rising seas?

Turn off the lights when you leave a room.

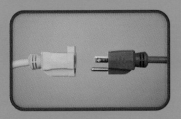

Electronics and chargers use power when they are plugged in—even when the device isn't in use. Unplug your chargers and devices when you're finished using them.

Healthy wetlands help prevent flooding. Find out if there are wetland restoration projects in your area and get involved.

Trees and other plants remove heat-trapping carbon dioxide from the air and soak up rainwater. Plant new trees in your yard or community garden.

Direct rainwater from your home's gutters and drains into rain barrels. This way you can use the water later rather than having it run into overflowing waterways.

Glossary

absorbs takes in or soaks up

atmosphere layers of gases that surround Earth

barrier islands long, sandy islands near a shore that stop some serious weather and flooding

carbon dioxide a gas given off when fossil fuels are burned

climate the typical weather in a place

climate refugees people who have been forced to leave their homes, towns, or countries because of the effects of climate change

deltas pieces of land often shaped like a triangle that are formed when rivers split into smaller rivers before flowing into the ocean

erosion the wearing away of rocks, soil, and sand by natural forces such as the movement of water and wind

fossil fuels fuels such as coal, oil, and gas made from the remains of plants and other organisms that died millions of years ago

glaciers huge areas of ice and snow found on mountains and near the North and South Poles

high tides the times when seawaters are at their highest levels and come farthest up on land

nuisance something that is annoying or causes problems

reefs chains of rocks, coral, or sand that lie near the surface of a body of water

surges rises of water due to a storm or hurricane

wetlands areas of land, such as marshes or swamps, where soil is usually covered by shallow water

Read More

Blake, Kevin. *Houston's Hurricane Harvey Floods (Code Red).* New York: Bearport Publishing, 2019.

Kurtz, Kevin. *Climate Change and Rising Sea Levels (Searchlight Books: Climate Change).* Minneapolis: Lerner Publications, 2019.

London, Martha. *Stopping Climate Change (Climate Change).* Minneapolis: Abdo Publishing, 2021.

Thomas, Keltie. *Rising Seas: Flooding, Climate Change, and Our New World.* Buffalo, NY: Firefly Books, 2018.

Learn More Online

1. Go to **www.factsurfer.com** or scan the QR code below.

2. Enter "**Rising Seas**" into the search box.

3. Click on the cover of this book to see a list of websites.

Index

animals 22–23

atmosphere 6, 26, 28

carbon dioxide 6, 28–29

climate change 10, 18, 24, 26, 28

erosion 4, 22, 26

flood barriers 20, 26, 27

fossil fuels 6, 26, 28

glaciers 6, 8, 13

global warming 15

high tides 16, 18, 20, 22

hurricanes 18, 25

melting 8, 10, 13

nuisance flooding 16–17

plants 20, 22–23, 29

sea level 10, 12, 14–16, 20, 22–24, 26, 28

storms 18

storm surge 18, 20, 22, 27

tides 16, 18, 20, 22

wetlands 20, 26, 29

About the Author

Raymond Bergin is a writer living in New Jersey. Though his home is an hour's drive from the shore, he is no stranger to high water. In 2021, the remnants of Hurricane Ida dumped 10 inches (25 cm) of rain on his property within 5 hours. Nearby creeks and streams overflowed and left him with a flooded basement.